Baby Philosophers

Baby Philosophers

SYDNIE MICHELE

RUNNING PRESS
PHILADELPHIA • LONDON

9   8   7   6   5   4   3   2   1
Digit on the right indicates the number of this printing

Library of Congress Cataloging-in-Publication Number 00-135508

ISBN 0-7624-0960-6

Cover and interior design by Terry Peterson
Edited by Molly Jay
Typography: Wendy, New Caledonia, Calligraphic 421

This book may be ordered by mail from the publisher.
Please include $2.50 for postage and handling.

But try your bookstore first!

Running Press Book Publishers
125 South Twenty-second Street
Philadelphia, Pennsylvania 19103-4399

Visit us on the web!
www.runningpress.com

Acknowledgments

Rarely does anyone accomplish anything worthwhile alone,
and there are many people to thank. But the heart of my
gratitude deservedly goes to my husband and partner
Stephen Salmieri, virtuoso photographer. He was there
for me at every photo session and it was his
participation that allowed me the freedom
to create, a wonderful gift.

Dedication

Lovingly dedicated to Danielle, Darryl, Halle, and Ethan—my favorite philosophers.

Introduction

As a portrait photographer, I have always found babyhood a visually fascinating and provocative subject. Though babies can be a daunting subject (after all, they accept no art direction), for me they are a charmed source of inspiration. In a world where far too much that comes before our eyes is harsh and slick or confusing and false, babies are simple, honest, and pure.

I find that my lens and my eye are easily seduced by nursling ardor. Initially I was taken by the beauty and natural symmetry of the infant's form. Their bodies are round and firm, yet buttery soft at the same time. They come with plum dimpled hands, wispy curls at the nape of the neck, little rosebud mouths and luminous eyes that steadily follow your each and every movement. Babies are the only people on whom rolls of fat actually look good, and it is the only legal time in life when one can run naked and free. I love the puckishness of these spirited playfellows, and I delight in their nascent sense of humor. But most of all, these new ones have a transparency of personality that is lost in adult subjects, making them a most engaging theme for portraiture. Smitten by these wide-eyed innocents, I knew I had found my subject.

While photography is for me an intentional and organized process, collecting quotes was a far more capricious affair. When I read or heard something that resonated truth and beauty for me, I quickly scribbled it down. My intention at this point was not to employ these insightful adages, but merely to explain to myself the meaning of life. Clarity on a scrap of paper, that's what I wanted. I wound up with a cache box full of aphorisms that eventually grew into a mound. I wrote them on index cards, pink and yellow sticky papers, or even a torn envelope flap.

Eventually a call to order prevailed. Categories appeared in my quote collection and major themes emerged. Duly noted were art and artists, philosophy and meaning, and what used to be called virtue (or, how to behave yourself). All were popular "sites" in my analog box. I didn't care if they were articulated yesterday, a hundred or a thousand years ago. They qualified if they were timeless and relevant, and especially if combined with a bit of levity

New parents are the proudest people and my studio was filled with a happy procession of infant geniuses. These little ones frequently struck angel poses, which so impressed me that I took no notice of the crooked path my muse was leading me on. The comic and preposterous photographs seen here were not figured into the equation. While the mounting collection of images in *Baby Philosophers* came as a surprise to me, I suspect this was not so for the newborns who always seem to know when they are contributing to a higher purpose.

When it comes to politics, babies are supreme statesmen. But unlike politicians, babies are absolutely no good at hiding their feelings. They will move seamlessly from delirious pleasure to screaming rage. Even the cutest bambino will metamorphose into a gargoyle, only to rejoin us moments later with tear-stained laughter. The naked personality arising from these little beings must have inspired Ralph Waldo Emerson to pen: "Infancy conforms to nobody; all conform to it."

Thus, I have found that even the most carefully orchestrated photo session, including Mozart in the background (the preferred musical choice of babydom) can easily disintegrate into chaos and frequently did. I contemplated this as I clicked away on my camera.

With more and more frequency, I was beginning to see the absurd and the goofy appear on my contact sheets. Initially I paid little attention these anomalies, as they did not fit the description of my self-appointed mission of truth and beauty. Increasingly, however, the incongruous photograph caught my interest and I felt compelled to apply the red china marker to these images jumping out at me from my proofs. Although these selections embarrassed me at first, I was buttressed by the voice of poet Alan Ginsberg who wisely advised: "When the muse calls, answer." I did!

I don't recall the exact moment that provoked the serendipitous mingling of the Yoda-like baby characters with the formidable profundities of their elders, but I do remember how I howled with laughter as my eyes were finally opened to the wacky creation of *Baby Philosophers* I had been gestating for years unbeknownst to myself!

As the first few pairings of quotes and faces instantly found each other, the choice of what to do became clear.

My perverse muse was satisfied at last when an initial "cut and paste" left no doubt that this potpourri of infant protégés was indeed illustrating the wisdom of the ages. In fact, the absurd association helped adhere the quotation to memory.

Babies are the freshest human beings around. When adults grow stale you'll be glad of their company. Babies are unpredictable, uninhibited, never pretentious, frequently courageous and endlessly energetic. They are always ready to play or eat or sleep or poop with the same enthusiasm that adults reserve only for "important" events. Babies know how to just be, and they love to teach us that skill. Writer Lin Yutang tells us what every baby knows: "If you cannot spend a perfectly useless afternoon in a perfectly useless manner, you have not learned how to live."

Whenever you have a spare moment, play with a baby. They are the most amiable playmates and they most kindly bestow that playfulness on us.

Babies light the world. They are connected to everyone everywhere. Babies are born to generate love.

Syndie Michele

When we are born, we cry
that we are come to this
great stage of fools.

WILLIAM SHAKESPEARE

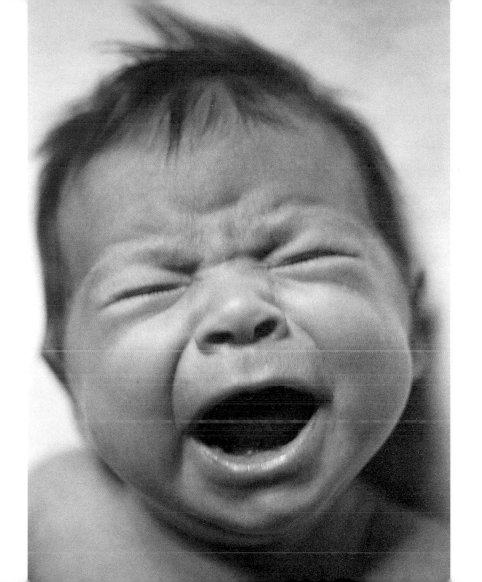

In merciless and rollicking comedy, life is caught in the act.

GEORGE SANTAYANA

Life must be lived forwards, but can only be understood backwards.

SOREN KIERKEGAARD

Oh happy is he who can still hope to rise out of this flood of errors.

JOHANN WOLFGANG VON GOETHE

Art is whatever you can get away with.

MARCEL DUCHAMP

Without music, life would be a mistake.

FRIEDRICH NIETZSCHE

There's really nothing to it, all you have to do is hit the right notes at the right time and the instrument plays itself.

J.S. BACH

A bird does not sing
because he has an answer.
He sings because
he has a song.

JOAN WALSH ANGLUND

Get it 'till it's perfect
then cut two minutes.

FRED ASTAIRE

The artistic temperament
is a disease that
afflicts amateurs.

C.K. CHESTERTON

To have arrived is
to be in prison.

HENRI MATISSE

Mistakes are the portals of discovery.

JAMES JOYCE

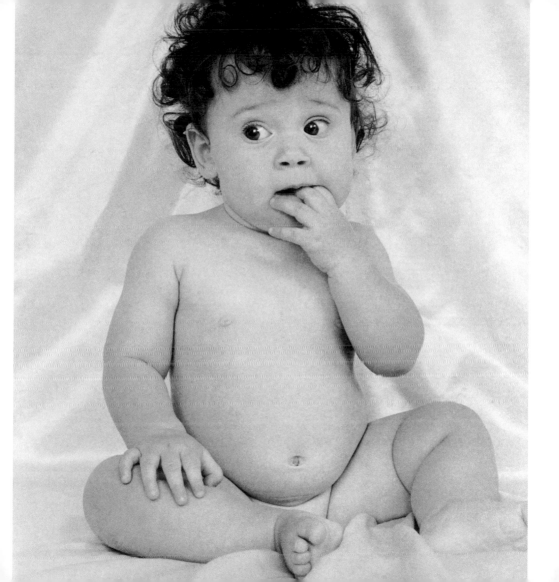

*Life is a tragedy
when seen in close up,
but a comedy in long shot.*

CHARLIE CHAPLIN

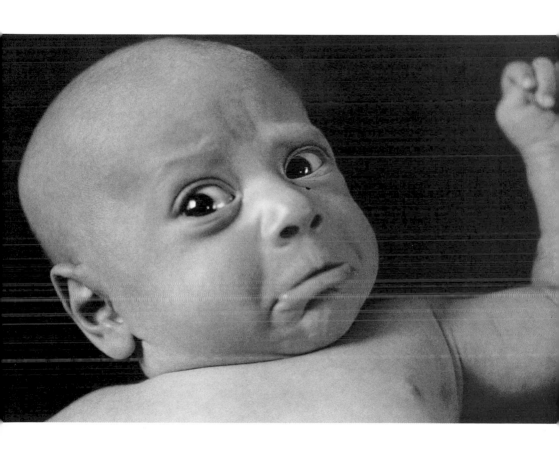

Those who know don't tell.
Those who tell don't know.

A ZEN SAYING

Great spirits have always encountered violent opposition from mediocre minds.

ALBERT EINSTEIN

Question authority!
Think for yourself.

TIMOTHY LEARY

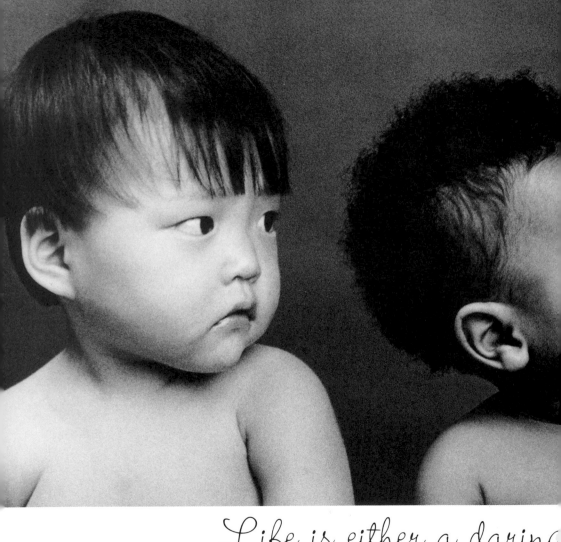

Life is either a daring

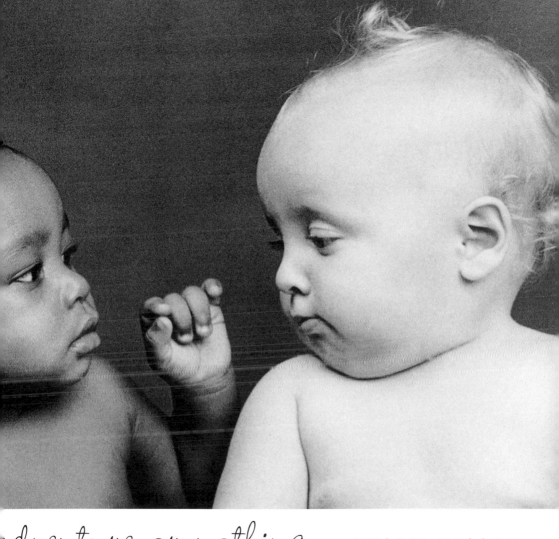

dventure or nothing. HELEN KELLER

Humor is the only divine quality of man.

ARTHUR SCHOPENHAUER

Nothing is more hopeless than a scheme of merriment.

SAMUEL JOHNSON

I have often
regretted my speech,
never my silence.

PUBLILUS

The naked truth
is still taboo.

BOB DYLAN

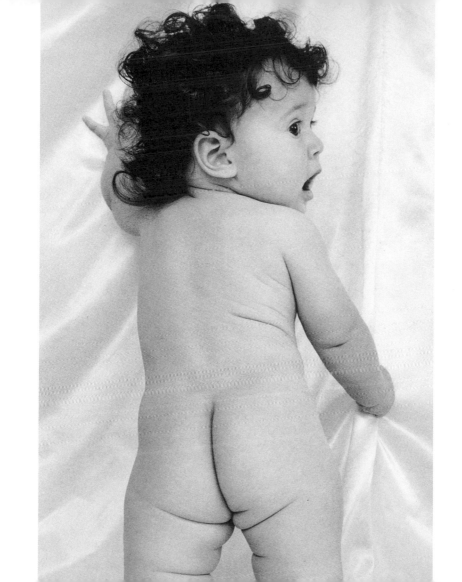

It takes two to
speak the truth,
one to speak
and one to hear.

HENRY DAVID THOREAU

The most useless day
of all is that in which
we have not laughed.

SEBASTIAN R.N. CHAMPORT

Beware of all enterprises that require new clothes.

HENRY DAVID THOREAU

The less you need
the freer you become.

E. F. SCHUMACHER

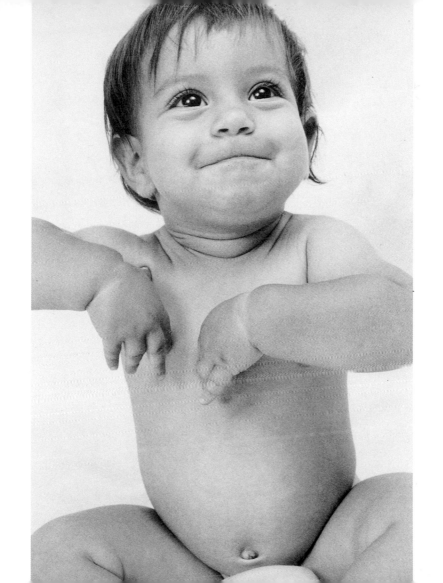

The unexamined life
is not worth living.

PLATO

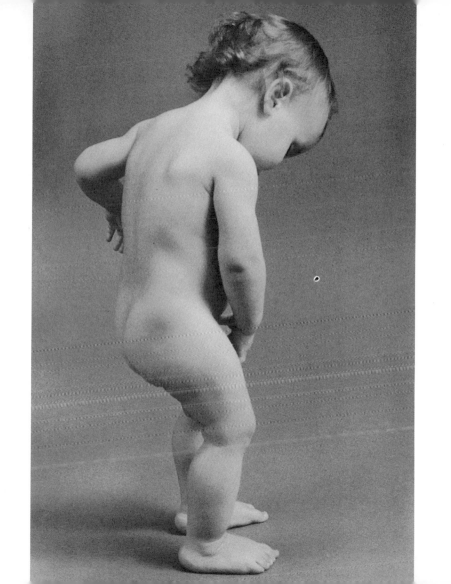

It's not that there are no more clowns, it's just that people have forgotten how to laugh.

FEDERICO FELLINI

A beautiful woman should break her mirror early.

BALTASAR GRACIAN

The innocent and the beautiful
have no enemy but time.

W.B. YATES

You cannot prevent the birds of sadness from passing over your head, but you can prevent them from making nests in your hair.

CHINESE PROVERB

Not a shred of evidence occurs in favor of the idea that life is serious.

BRENDAN GILL

The days that make us happy make us wise.

JOHN MAESFIELD

Walking on water wasn't
built in a day.

JACK KEROUAC

Make haste slowly.

EDGAR CAYCE

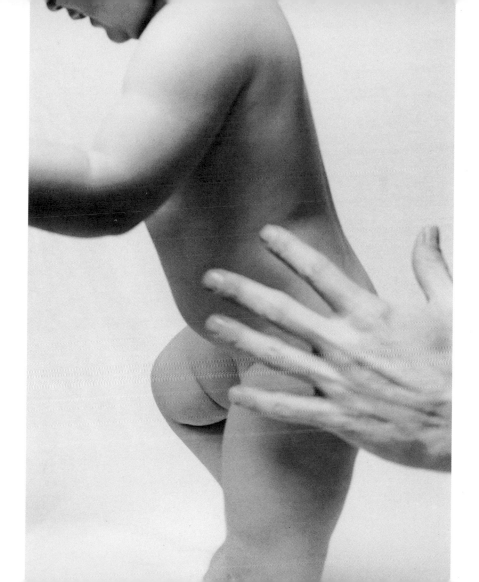

*What you do not want
done to yourself
do not do to others.*

CONFUCIUS

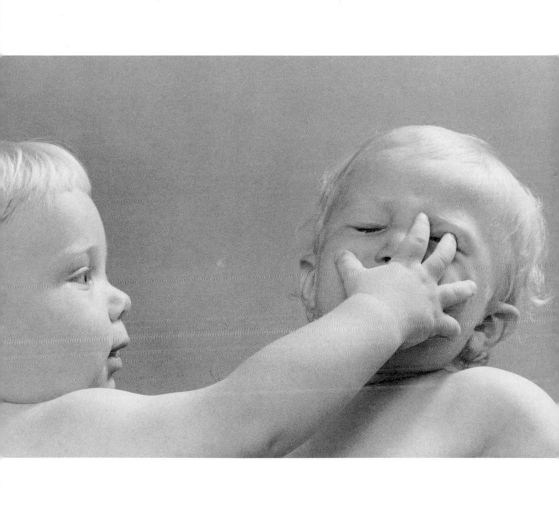

The goal of action
is contemplation.

ARISTOTLE

*Life is not a spectacle,
or a feast,
it's a predicament.*

GEORGE SANTAYANA

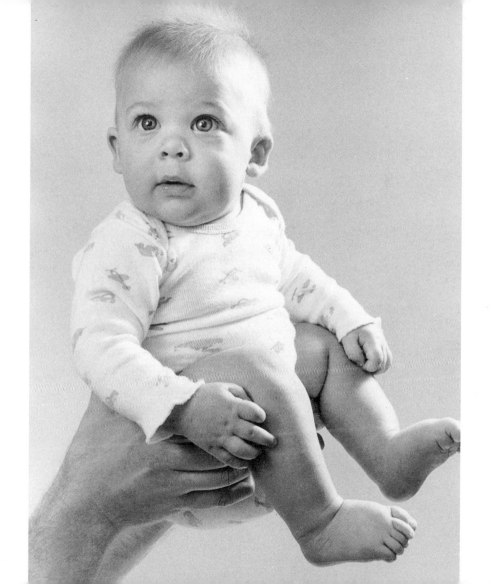

The real voyage of discovery
consists not in seeking
new landscapes,
but in having new eyes.

MARCEL PROUST

He who knows he has a
enough, is rich.

LAO TSU

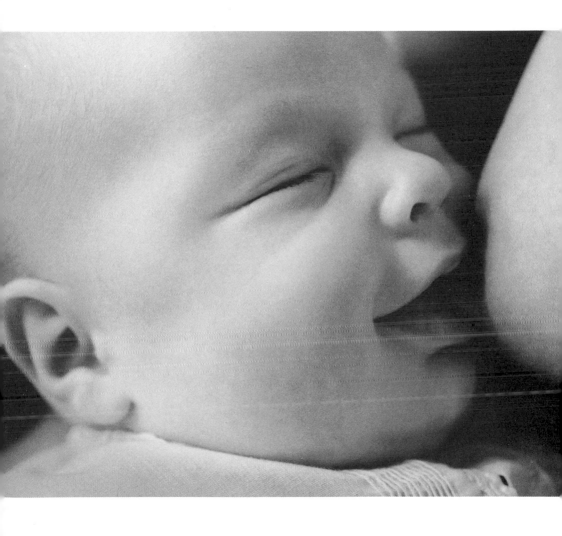

There is no reciprocity.
Men love women.
Women love children.
Children love hamsters.

ALICE THOMAS ELLIS

I hate quotations.

RALPH WALDO EMERSON

*A picture is worth a
thousand bucks.*

CECIL BEATON